THE
SAVAGE
STYLE

JONATHAN SAVAGE

THE SAVAGE STYLE

Gibbs Smith

For my beloved parents, Judy and Larry Savage, whose brilliance,
drive, creativity, curiosity, dedication to our whole family, and devotion
to each other and to finding the joy in your life's work together
inspire me every day. Your boundless support, endless encouragement,
and unshakeable belief will always fuel my determination to think big,
dream bigger, and continue to aim for excellence.
I couldn't be more grateful.

CONTENTS

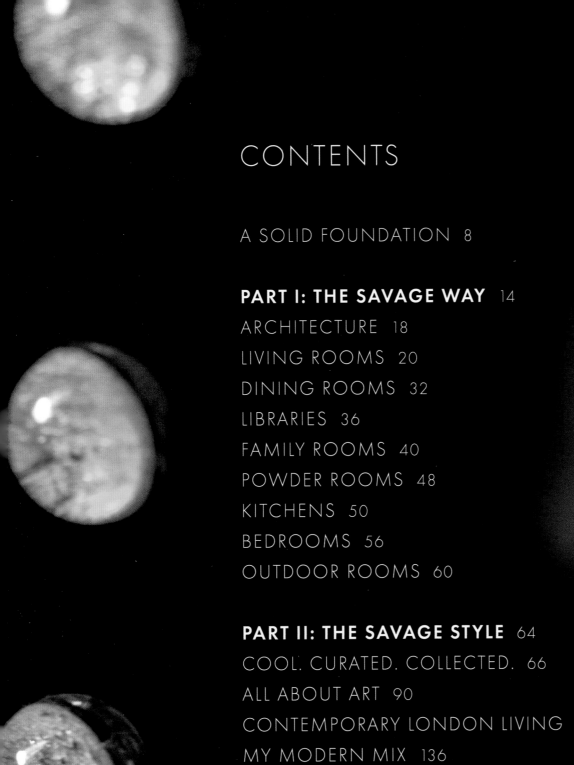

A SOLID FOUNDATION

In the South, we're famously house proud. We entertain at home. We believe we know a thing or two about how to make a house welcoming, comfortable, and beautiful—a home, in other words. We also believe that every home should express the family's personality, and reflect their history, spirit, and passions. Obviously, all of us live in our own way, even though the basic outlines of our lives may be the same in terms of our everyday activities at home. Yet the person who hosts dinner parties twice or three times a month has one lifestyle, while the person who never gives a party has another, and the person who entertains on a large scale still another. But regardless, the rooms always need to function for that person's or that family's purpose, which means they should be designed in a manner that's complementary to their lifestyle. As an interior designer, of course, I hold this truth to be self-evident. My job as I see it is to create unique spaces—spaces that express the personality and character of each family, that capture their specific tastes, preferences, and dreams, but above all, that work for the way they plan to use them.

I am a fan of intimate spaces where people can enjoy their conversations, so I'll take expansive, elegant rooms and divide them into smaller, convivial, interesting spaces. I want people to have conversations in settings that bring them just the right amount of closeness to one another so they can laugh and share ideas and stories. There should always be a convenient spot to sit and a place to set down a drink. Whether people are in a room with seating for twenty or for four, they should be comfortable—and comfort is individual. This is why communication is everything. The better I know the families I design for, the more deeply I understand what they're looking for, and the more their home will suit their personalities, needs, and dreams in the end.

I am a fast-paced New Yorker at heart, living in the South. I'm constantly on a plane and eager to see what's new but also always happy to come home to Nashville. I travel like mad for the love of it. It's inspiring, and it's also part of my DNA as a designer to be out in the world on the hunt for special, unusual, exceptional things for my clients that no one else has or has ever seen—that woven carpet from Nepal drenched in colors you can drown in, that hand-embroidered cloth from Dubrovnik that shows the tradition of centuries. No matter how often I'm in London, Paris, or Milano, I always unearth something new, whether it's a leather-wrapped piece by Jacques Adnet, a collection of Keith Murray ceramics for Wedgwood, or mid-century lighting blown on Murano. But as much as I love those cities, I also am wildly curious to see the wider world and its places, secret and not so secret, that are on and off the beaten track, as both a design-obsessed tourist and an open-eyed explorer. That said, I was raised on a farm in Livingston, Tennessee. Growing up in a small town in rural America where everyone knows everyone else and their grandmother means absolutely everything to me. And since Livingston is just two hours from Nashville, I had the best of both worlds—city and country—from an early age.

Somedays I think I was born to be a designer. I certainly have houses in my blood because both my parents are in real estate. My father has developed countless residential properties. He is always building something, so the smell of lumber, the sound of hammering nails, and the idea of something being created and constructed has always been a part of who I am. My mother is a real estate agent who loves houses and often sold many of my father's projects. From the time I was a small child, I used to rearrange the living room, dragging furniture across my mom's hardwood floors, which inevitably needed refinishing when I was done.

The house I grew up in was a conglomeration of things passed down from both sides of the family. And in terms of decorating, my mom had the notion that more is more. My design aesthetic is just not that. After living eighteen years in an environment that was a hodgepodge of antiques and family heirlooms, less became more for me, even before I began studying interior design seriously. I started out in international business in college, but during my time abroad in London, I switched into the interior design program at the American University in London. When I moved back to Nashville, I put international business aside for good and enrolled at O'More College of Design in Franklin, Tennessee, now known as the O'More School of Architecture & Design at Belmont University.

In my time as a design student, I was fortunate to know the legendary Albert Hadley, a fellow proud Tennessean (his middle name was Livingston, like my hometown) who, as a partner in the New York-based interior design firm Parish-Hadley, transformed the perception, the look, and the legacy of interior design in America. Consequently, after graduation, I decided I wanted to be a New Yorker. Mr. Hadley introduced me to David Kleinberg, a Parish-Hadley alum with a modernist bent in whose office I worked for the next few years. One of the most important lessons I learned there was that interiors should always be appropriate for the people, the place, and the time—or, as Kleinberg likes to say, "No silk ballgowns at the beach."

The other highlight of my time in New York was meeting my life partner, Bradley Wensel, a business executive. When Brad was offered a wonderful opportunity in Nashville, we moved back to the Music City, and I opened my own firm. Ten years later, I opened my second office in Palm Beach, Florida. We've traveled back and forth between the two since then with our dog Artie, a Lagotto Romagnolo (Italian truffle hunter), who is the joy and light of our lives.

I realize that creating a home is a major investment, so I want to make sure that each one that I design works for the people who live in it. In my view, rooms only come alive when people use them, so I'm not a fan of spaces that don't draw people in every day. In my house growing up, some rooms were never used, and others only when company was over or for special occasions. Today, the families I design for want to live in every square inch of their homes. My goal is to implement choices that make their spaces functional, interesting, creative, and above all, enjoyable and enduring.

There are classic design principles that drive my thinking whether the home is traditional or modern. I believe the architecture of the home should drive the overall aesthetic throughout. But that said, sometimes the fun is the mix, and the home that's traditional on the exterior may become its best self with the unexpected: an interior that's clean, transitional, or more contemporary.

Geography matters, too, because the quality of light is obviously different from location to location, which affects the color palette. In South Florida, colors need to be perfect because the sunlight is so vivid. In London, where it's often gray and rainy, we might construct a more upbeat, happy interior to contrast the gloominess of the weather. In Los Angeles, I usually take a more tonal approach because the sunlight is not as direct. In the mountains, everything changes because the light reflects off the snow in the winter, and the colors of the surrounding plants, trees, and earth come forward in the spring and summer. Our home in Palm Beach is just one example of what I mean. We did a soothing, neutral interior there, with almost no color, because of the vivid blue skies and green palm and sea grape trees outside the window. Why would I even try to compete against Mother Nature when I know she's always going to win?

The same idea of appropriateness applies to fabrics as well. Some feel destined for certain environments and not for others, whether it's wool bouclé in the mountains or linen at the beach. In New York, I might use a lot of velvet and elegant fabrics. I probably wouldn't use the same scheme in the country, in the city, and on the coast. The instinct for the right fabric for the right place is now a part of my nature.

I'm a tactile person and partial to clothes and fashion, so I have a passion for texture and fabrics, especially fine apparel fabrics like linens, cottons, cashmere, silk, and other natural woven materials. (I dress most of the upholstery I design in men's suiting fabrics.) But I couldn't live without today's performance fabrics—I use them all the time—because they're engineered not just for durability and easy maintenance, but also to just feel wonderful on the skin.

I also love color. And while I don't necessarily live in a lot of color, when a client wants color, we do color proud. I know the power lighting has in a home. Dramatic lighting overhead can change a space, make it more interesting, and make it feel taller because it draws the eye up to the ceiling.

This is all to say that I customize each interior to the specific persona and family so their homes look like them, and not like anyone else. It's hard work to do what's different, but the different, individual, and unique is what's important to me and to the creativity that I think lies at the heart and soul of my profession. The drive to make something never seen before that's just perfect for its purpose has propelled me to work with so many talented craftspeople and artisans over the years: old-world upholsterers who know how to build comfort that lasts for all different styles of rooms and, more important, all different body types; glass artists who can blow, carve, etch, mirror, and back-paint functional works of beauty for lighting, backsplashes, tabletops, and so much more; master carpenters and metal workers who know how to fine tune and forge the traditions of their artisanry into furniture and stair rails and so many other elements of the interior landscape that contribute to the scenery of a home and make it remarkable; painters who use centuries-old traditions of fine finishing to transform a room's vertical surfaces and overhead planes into works of twenty-first-century art.

Of course, I also shop a lot, because shopping is really one of my passions in life, and in one sense, it's why I do what I do. I get on a plane to Paris at least twice a year to put my nose to the ground and find what no one else has. There's always so much out there. And I've found that wherever you go, if you dig in, you'll find something special, so why not make the most of the opportunity and treat it like a treasure hunt?

I want to do what I know will make my clients proud. When people say, "Tell me what you think I need," that's a limitless task at hand. My team and I will stock the pantry. We'll do the china, the linens, the glassware, the bedding, the towels, you name it, if that's what that family wants and needs. If the person is a collector, we'll be on the lookout for things to add to their holdings or suggest something new that might appeal. The point is to try to give people not just what they want, but what they don't know they want.

Everything in life depends on relationships. Trust matters. This is especially true in interior design because the process of creating a home is complex and a major investment of time and resources. I foster the trust I need to exceed my clients' expectations by assuring them that my team and I have the expertise, that their floor plan works, that a set of dimensions is exact, and that rooms function differently depending on which decisions and choices they make. The back and forth of the design process, of giving people options, of showing what works and why, is what ultimately builds the relationship. Once you do that, you build a rapport—and in my experience, building rapport is building the interior.

PAGE 8: For me, fashion, art, and design go hand in hand, just like they did in my stairway for the New York Kips Bay Decorator Show House in 2017. OPPOSITE: I practice what I preach at home, too.

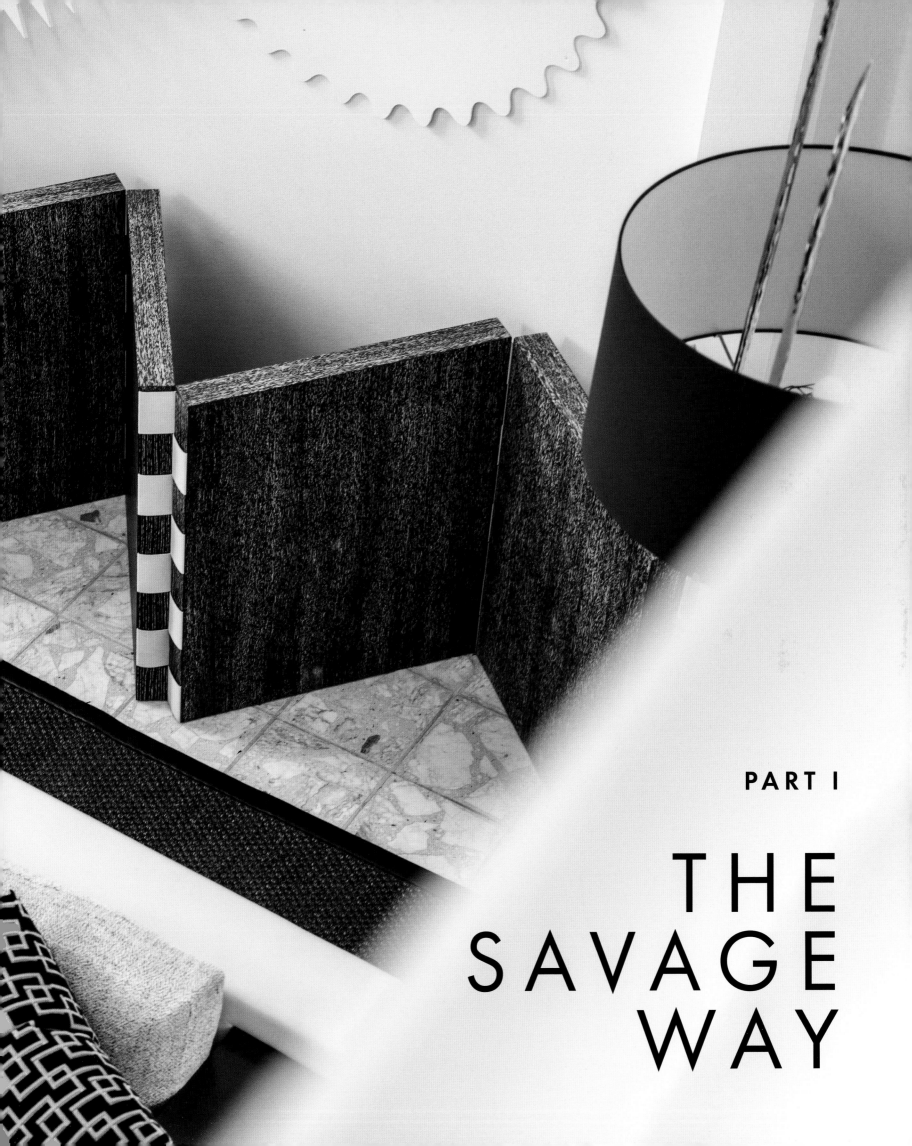

PART I

THE SAVAGE WAY

Yes, I believe each home should reflect its owners and bring them joy every day. Yes, I work to make each home comfortable and appropriate for its function, location, and architecture. And yes, my ultimate goal is to create homes that are so individual, unique, and beautiful that my clients are delighted to share, and no one ever wants to leave. But what does that mean in terms of design? To me, it's the belief that every home should flow together as one fully conceived entity. Each room should have its own identity, function and comfort should take precedence, and details should sing. This may sound paradoxical, but, believe me, it's not. And it is why I tend to design each home from the front door to the back door.

Design gives us so many different means and tools to create the feeling of connectedness. There are ways of taking certain colors and adding complementary colors and patterns to weave a visual thread throughout the house that the eye appreciates and makes sense of. The same can be done with textures, materials, or graphic moments—or some combination of all these elements. It's this cohesiveness, whatever the look or style, that makes a house feel like a home. I like to do more with less. But I believe that the classical principles of design—balance, harmony, form, proportion, scale, repetition, contrast—are foundational, enduring, and immutable. And I follow them, always, even when I break what other people consider to be the rules.

PRECEDING OVERLEAF: In my Nashville living room, scale, proportion, and finish bring the bold graphic elements into balance so the room is visually serene. OPPOSITE: Creamy matte, paneled walls create a quiet but activated backdrop that sets off the materials and forms of standout pieces like Joann Westwater's mirror-inlaid cabinet and a gunmetal-striped ceramic vase purchased in London.

ARCHITECTURE

The architecture of the house, the location, and the purpose—is it a primary residence or a vacation retreat?—set the outlines for my decision-making process. Of course, there's nothing better than having the opportunity to improve the scale, proportion, flow, and architectural detail. And it's how I begin a project whenever possible. But that said, my approach is to work from the inside out. I tend to start with the fabrics and build the color schemes based off the fabric choices. But before we select fabrics, we lay out the furniture plan for each room. Once that's done, we place the fabrics on the pieces. Then we build each room with wall and ceiling finishes. And then we ground everything with the carpet. But I love to begin with fabrics, since that is what my clients touch and respond to the most.

But let's begin at the front door. The most important room in a home in my view is the foyer or entry hall. This space is the place of first impressions, the perfect opportunity to set the tone and mood for the entire house, so why not make it as impactful as possible? The entry provides the perfect opportunity to accentuate details—from a beautiful handmade stair railing or an unusual carpet to an eye-catching work of art—to clue everyone into what they can expect ahead. Depending on the scale, the size, and the overall feeling desired, this space can be fun, fabulous, or functional. But it's here that the flow begins. Suppose, for example, the choice is to use a relatively neutral palette of white with black. In each subsequent room, I may pull in black and white to a degree, but I will also feed in a third color that changes from room to room. For me, the foyer is the welcome mat of rooms, and I want the rest of the house to live up to this starting moment.

The swoops and sweeps of this plaster-finished Nashville entry hall afforded us the opportunity to give the expected traditional elements a slight modern twist. All the decorative choices— the custom, hand-forged iron stair railing, center hall table with its iron base, and curved settee beneath the paintings by Charlotte Terrell—take their cues from the architectural envelope.

LIVING ROOMS

The living room is another of a home's most important rooms. As such, it needs to be comfortable, stylish, and designed for conviviality. In most homes, this room is where we gather with friends and spend time together in conversation. It's also the place where families sit together and make memories. My mother always hosted company in the living room, which was decorated to the nines. Today, living rooms tend to be more casual and much more comfortable than the one I remember from my childhood, which means families can use them all the time instead of just for special occasions.

Successful living rooms today are all about seating. In my experience, everyone prefers to have their own individual seat or chair. Long sofas may look fabulous, but they're just like the back seats of cars: no one wants to sit in the middle. Depending on how the space is contrived, a four pack of chairs around an ottoman works like a charm. A sofa with a pair of chairs can be just as inviting. Multiple seating groups? That's a question answered by the room's dimensions. As to the degree of firmness, percentage of down, seat heights and depths, armless, low arm, or high arm, I encourage my clients to make these decisions. What's comfortable for me may not be comfortable for you. When we're doing custom upholstery, I make sure the client tries out different options to understand their preferences. It's also important that children and pets are taken into account. In today's world, you can use performance fabrics and scrub everything you want. There are incredible performance surfaces, more than ever before: vinyls that feel like leather, carpets that are pet safe and clean up with soap and water, and so on. If kids and animals are part of the family, make sure to tell your designer.

But my first focus is on the seating in the living room, which includes handy surfaces and little tables nearby to put down a drink, a book, or hold a lamp—and the occasional piano. It's fun, especially during the holidays, to gather people together to listen to someone play—or in Nashville, to sing. It's also key to have different levels of light to be able to adjust for the time of day and the function. Whether it's a winter afternoon by the fireplace with beautiful dim lamp lighting or a cocktail party or fundraiser where overall ambient lighting makes sense, I'll include a variety of sources to maximize flexibility and mood. Living rooms are also a great place to showcase art because whatever the art is—a painting, installation, or sculpture—it becomes a launching point for conversation and contemplation.

This Nashville living room inspired by the Dior shop in Paris updates tradition with unexpected contemporary touches, like the bold Studio Van Den Akker coffee table; subtly luxurious flourishes such as the Maison Jansen side table, Holland & Sherry pillows, and gilded Paul Ferrante stools; and a symphonic play of matte textures and shine in lacquer, rock crystal, and shagreen.

The windows that bring the outside into this Atlanta study informed many of the furnishing decisions. Lounge chairs by Julian Chichester and the stone-topped table from Ironware International—called "The Jonathan," one of my designs and inspired by a Givenchy table—pick up on their black outlines. OVERLEAF LEFT: The bookshelf is an essay in display with its groupings of black glass and rock crystal objects, books wrapped in handmade Japanese paper, and a collection of interesting geometric fractal forms found in Paris. OVERLEAF RIGHT: A trio of decorative mirrors by Mark Evans through Ainsworth-Noah add a brooch-like fashion touch of jewelry.

From the stenciled floors painted by Jason Duran to the chevron banding, nailhead trim, and striped contrast cording, details, details, details bring the zing to this otherwise neutral Franklin, Tennessee, living room.

The delicate tracery of Paul Ferrante's twig-and-vine-inspired pieces adds just the right grace notes of decorative ornament into the essentially geometric forms that compose this serene living room in Belle Mead. A collection of Roy Hamilton vases draws the eye to the built-in cabinets that flank the chimney breast.

ABOVE: The muted glow of brass, onyx, parchment, and gilding set off an artwork by Alexander Calder.
RIGHT: Curves meeting angles is an essential design conversation. BELOW LEFT: Platinum-painted, hand-carved chair feet bring functional jewelry to the floor.
BELOW RIGHT: Rock crystal obelisks feel especially elemental on a marble slab.

LEFT: This coffee table brings a needed graphic jolt. RIGHT: What's more glamorous than a crystal chandelier, transformed? BELOW: Maison Jansen's brass and burl wood chest anchors this grouping. BELOW RIGHT: Horsehair wallpaper sets off the bold forms. BOTTOM: Every room benefits from a nature reference.

DINING ROOMS

Dining rooms in my view are almost born to serve a variety of functions. Of course, dinner parties are the heart of the matter. But a dining room can be a fabulous place to play cards or board games or have a wine tasting. For the kids to do homework. For you and the kids to lay out a craft or an art project. Or to convert to a great work-from-home space should that become necessary. The point is that a large tabletop gives you the real estate on which to do almost anything you want. This makes lighting crucial for all the obvious reasons. Multiple sources—overhead, wall fixtures, tabletop, and ambient—are important because they give the flexibility to create different moods. And adjustability matters because various activities and types of occasions call for different levels of illumination. If you're playing cards, for example, you want more and brighter light than if you're giving a dinner party. And if you're working from home, you need total control.

Anything—well, almost anything—goes in a dining room décor-wise. I've always thought of this room as a natural home for a scenic paper. Or hand-painted panels. Or lacquer, depending on the space and the scale. But I always want to do more than just paint the walls and ceiling because I think a dining room is a gathering place, and rooms where people come together command a more thought-out, finished, and finessed surface treatment. This is partly because dining can be a celebration, and thus involve a bit of theater. But it's also because the dining room is a space where all our senses come into play, and as such, we should make the effort to please them.

Dining rooms deserve all the decorative drama we can give them. Here, the lacquer chairbacks and bronze table sculpture speak to the mirror's traditional tracery in a contemporary mode. The silver-leafed ceiling shimmers above the droplets of Ochre's modern chandelier. The Rug Co.'s Shadow carpet grounds the ethereal elements, and Maison Jansen's ebonized oval pedestals almost suggest structural columns.

The raw elmwood beams of this Nashville dining room set the stage for its play of rustic versus refined. Grass cloth walls balance the sophistication of the curtains in a Clarence House silk and the antiqued mirrored panels behind the buffet. The hand-forged iron base of the French white oak–topped table keeps the room open enough so that nothing feels too heavy.

LIBRARIES

Libraries are one of my favorite rooms to design. For me, they're an extension of the living room, with everything that entails design-wise, plus all your favorite books. I have a serious literary habit of my own, so I am always experimenting with ways to corral my never-ending holdings into a pleasing, functional order. And I am always grateful and intrigued to explore different ways of displaying my clients' collections. Sometimes the books are completely visible; other times, they're totally hidden. The solution depends on what my clients have in mind. I generally include a small desk, a beautiful seating arrangement, and a game table in the libraries I design. Tradition has it that the walls should be paneled, and that's always an option. However, I've finished the walls in everything from beautiful leather to wood paneling to lacquer, and not every room needs that or is of that ilk. What libraries do require is comfortable seating, and preferably a choice of spots to settle in and read. In addition, these are intimate rooms in which one can have a quiet drink and conversation, gather for cocktails prior to dinner depending on the size of the party, or top off the evening with a nightcap.

In the interior landscape, libraries tend to be cocoons of all-embracing comfort, from wall finishes to the furnishings to the floor coverings. For this Nashville client, a red-headed fashionista, a library lacquered in Benjamin Moore's Hot Apple Spice felt like a natural fit. The custom-colored table by Martha Sturdy runs with the color story.

Shetland horsehair wall panels wrap this Nashville music room in an ombré embrace. The addition of a hand-applied pewter finish creates a crescendo of shimmer beneath the charcoal lacquered ceiling. Holland & Sherry embroidered pillows, crystal obelisks, a ceramic lamp, and hand-carved stools add important grace notes to the composition.

FAMILY ROOMS

The family room or den is what we in the South call the keeping room. This is the space, normally close to the kitchen, where everyone congregates while others are making dinner. The family room is meant to be a cozy, inviting place for the entire family, so it needs to incorporate enough seating for everyone at home plus overflow for guests. We use many different styles of seating for dining rooms. But in the family room or den, our go-to is a big, comfy sectional sofa and all sorts of cushy items, often leather- or faux-leather covered—think ottomans, club chairs, lounges—all with easy access to something suitable for putting your feet on. I like to design these rooms as if they're an extension of the kitchen or living room but always with my less-is-more casual approach.

Boxy geometries say it all in this family room. Cotton velvet–covered club chairs beckon to all who enter. A Christian Liaigre–designed tea table offers a handy surface for pretty objects, with dog toys stored in the basket below. The graphic table from Niermann Weeks, which hovers over a witty bronze faux bois box, adds sharp outlines into the mix.

Contrasting textures create intrigue and interest when the color palette tends to muted neutrals. Here, the ceiling beams and fireplace wall of ashlar limestone bring bold rusticity to the room's refined glass expanses, lime-washed walls, and Chanel pillow and throw. A sofa by Ferrell Mittman speaks to the classic contemporary forms of the club chairs. Side tables from Bill Sofield, lamps by Christopher Spitzmiller, and a Murano glass sculpture insert some softening curves.

This Nashville den is an exercise in updating tradition, with Bunny Williams's contemporary take on wing chairs, vintage leather-upholstered armchairs from Foxglove Antiques, columns and capitals from Architectural Artifacts, and Jack Lenor Larsen pillow fabric in a restrained pattern. OVERLEAF: A family gathering place, this Nashville game room features a balance of movable and fixed furnishings for various activities. Suzanne Kasler–designed chairs for Hickory Chair pull up to a Mattaliano games table. Woven-leather chairs from Mark Albrecht add to the flexibility. A light from Urban Electric hangs above the billiards table.

POWDER ROOMS

In my view, powder rooms are the one space in the home where we can let our imaginations run to fantasy and really show off a pattern, a color, or a true wall treatment. These rooms need to have personality. I work hard to create interesting powder rooms by breaking all the rules. So, anything goes in a powder room in my opinion.

ABOVE: Every powder room is an opportunity for fantasy. This burst of sunshine features a high-gloss ceiling, Barovier & Toso sconces, and Carleton V wallpaper. OPPOSITE: This graphic extravaganza is fun, unexpected, cheerful, and exciting. The custom countertop from Phoenix Granite & Marble balances Kelly Wearstler's bold wallpaper for Lee Jofa. Commissioned art by Ruby and Frank Stovesand adds just the right amount of color. The sconces are vintage.

KITCHENS

Kitchens are the heart of the home and usually the hardest working room. Some families have cooks to prepare meals. Other families cook for themselves. Sometimes, the kitchen needs to serve both styles of living. All of which makes the kitchen the ultimate multifunction room. Even more interesting is that the kitchen today is so often more than just one room. In many of the homes I design, it also includes a scullery, a pantry or walk-in pantry, a butler's pantry, or even a wet bar. My idea with kitchens and these ancillary spaces is to customize them as much as possible to accommodate the specific needs of that family. I always like to ensure there is a nice walkway around a cooktop so people aren't stepping over one another, but great bar seating might be just as important to my clients.

I personally love being in my kitchen. In the homes that we create we hope that the clients have the same feeling whether they're cooking, baking, doing meal prep, or setting up menus for entertaining. Color is so often a question in this space. We've done all white kitchens, all black kitchens, and run the gamut in between. With such beautiful, interesting, durable, easily cleanable materials available now, maintenance in this space is so much easier than it once was. We may use some less precious elements here than we do elsewhere in the house, but that's because kitchens are the ultimate utilitarian space, and we want them to be seriously functional as well as completely beautiful.

In this understated but highly considered kitchen, the detailing on the sides of the Cambria quartz island takes cues from the surrounding cabinetry. The curio is from Century Furniture; faucets are from Newport Brass; the vintage, 1950s poured-glass pendant is a find from Robin Rains Antiques.

ABOVE: From the Murano vase collection, metallic tiled backsplash, and silver-finished cabinets by Darryl Garrison to the Assemblage wallpaper and ceiling fixture from C L Sterling, fashion inspiration is everywhere in this glamorous bar. OPPOSITE: In this kitchen, symmetry plays a defining role. Pendant fixtures above the ample island reinforce the linear rhythms and add to the various textures that bring definition and visual interest to this essentially neutral kitchen. Robert Kuo's ceramic gourds add a lively sculptural presence to the island top.

There are white kitchens, and white kitchens. This capacious kitchen, designed with Vicki Edwards, a certified kitchen designer, is the second kind. Plank floors feel comfortable underfoot and set off the gentle figuring of the Calacatta Borghini marble countertops. Venetian plaster walls by Kevin Ansel wrap the room in a warm, elegant finish that quietly captures the light. English metal latticework on the cabinet fronts, pulls by E.R. Butler, and pendants by Vaughan bring the gleam and the glam.

BEDROOMS

My goal in bedrooms is always to create an oasis for the people who live in them, whether it's the heads of the house, a small child, or a grandparent. I believe every bedroom, including guest bedrooms, should incorporate all the comforts that we require to make resting a pleasure and all the considerations that we cherish when we're not feeling well. I like to include seating and a workspace, especially if there's not another area available. I can't think of anything more luxurious than beautiful custom bedding—I love a white bed—that complements the décor. Dressing rooms are also important to many of my clients, who cherish the beautiful items of apparel and accessories that they've collected over time. Many of them find their dressing room to be their happiest room, perhaps because it's the one room that's truly their own, and that we customized it just for their wants, needs, and preferences. Obviously, this space is an organizational challenge of a very high order given seasonal wardrobes and all that go with them. But dressing rooms tend to be the best kind of spatial algebra problems to solve, and so much fun to decorate. I don't think there's ever enough space allotted. And the bigger it is, the more apt we are to fill it.

This guest bedroom is a warm, welcoming retreat in beiges, burnt orange, and chocolate. An Hermès carpet and Roman shades in a Loro Piana linen bring the fashion forward. A Knoll textile upholsters the headboard. The table lamp by C L Sterling adds a touch of glass for sparkle.

This primary bedroom offers the homeowner a basically neutral retreat, with Venetian plaster walls enlivened by just enough pattern in the Osborne & Little fabric at the windows and draping the Calvin Klein four-poster bed to keep the eye engaged and interested. The bedside tables are from Hickory White; the sconces are from Christian Liaigre. A Mattaliano table centers the seating area.

OUTDOOR ROOMS

We approach outdoor rooms and outdoor living in the exact same way as we do indoor living spaces, except with more durable materials. This means we select everything from lamps, side tables, and seating to dining tables and draperies to create outdoor spaces that live like indoor spaces. The climate and our geographic location normally determine how much time we spend outside. In Florida, you can use outdoor spaces in the winter months, but not in the summer as comfortably. In the South, we can use our outdoor spaces nine months a year. In Maine, outdoor living is for summer only. That said, today's heaters, screens, draperies afford us the possibility of using those rooms for more seasons than ever before.

These ideas are all just an introduction to my approach and my foundational design principles, beliefs, and sensibilities filtered through my aesthetic lens. Making this philosophy manifest—that is, creating each home—requires an army of specialists with incredible expertise. I couldn't do any of what I do without the artisans, craftspeople, and vendors whose passion, vision, and business it is to make beauty. I'm only as strong as the people I employ. Having a coterie of people who do their utmost to turn my clients' thoughts and dreams into uniquely functional art for everyday living is vital. And in the South, in general, my clients get to know everyone who contributes to their homes. It's like building a whole other little family.

All the same design considerations apply to outdoor rooms as to indoor rooms, but durability and performance come even more to the fore. For this exterior living space, furnishings from Restoration Hardware with pillows in a Sunbrella stripe create seating areas with a strong visual presence and a bold graphic silhouette. Planters from Pennoyer Newman add even more flair.

Inspired by Christian Liaigre's home in St. Barts, this pool house in Palm Beach embodies the homeowner's idea of indoor-outdoor living. Teak furnishings from Sutherland, white furniture and planters from McKinnon and Harris, and limestone tile by Marmi Stone contribute to the overall relaxed elegance. Nathan Coe's photograph serves as a focal point and ties neatly into the surrounding palm trees.

PART II

THE
SAVAGE
STYLE

COOL. CURATED. COLLECTED.

I've always thought of show houses as gifts because they allow me to experiment with my design dreams. But participating in Kips Bay Decorator Show House Palm Beach in 2020 sparked a life dream. It brought in new projects, and with them, a yearning to return, work, and enjoy this natural getaway. I've long had a fascination with Eugene Lawrence, an architect who designed many of Palm Beach's more interesting modern buildings. When my partner and I found a place in one of his apartment houses from the 1970s and decided to gut the existing interior, we brought in Lawrence's talented son David to do the spatial development and architectural renderings.

The result is our ideal retreat. Its two bedrooms, incredible great room, a gallery-style entry hall, and wraparound terrace overlooking what locals call "the lake," the intercoastal waterway, let us work, relax, and entertain. I wanted to celebrate design as art here, so I filled it with many of my favorite things: lighting found at a Paris flea market and at auction in Los Angeles, an Hervé van der Straeten console, an Eric Schmitt console, pieces by Kimberly Denman made just for this apartment, and so many other special items by designers whose work I admire, everyone from Florence Knoll to Vladimir Kagan. This mix made the surroundings just right for choice pieces of art from our collection, including works by Josef Albers, Donald Judd, Victor Pasmore, George Williams, Ken Greenleaf, and others. I kept the palette light and neutral for the most part to not compete with the views, and I used mostly performance fabrics for ease of maintenance.

The art experience begins in the entry gallery, where artist Maria Apelo Cruz and I collaborated on the motif of the flora and fauna of South Florida to transform the walls. The design pays homage to the Beverly Hills Hotel's famous frond wallpaper, but Maria hand-piped plaster onto a linen background to create our diorama.

The great room encompasses the living space with its two seating areas, a lacquered bar with an églomisé backsplash I developed with the glass artist Miriam Ellner, and the dining area just around the corner where we entertain quite a bit. We kept these spaces in the neutral zone because of an incredible sea grape tree just outside the window that gives us so much greenery.

I love to cook, and so I designed myself the ultimate cook's kitchen. Wrapped in silver wallpaper and fitted out with Cosentino countertops, Gaggenau appliances, cream cerused-wood cabinets, this internal room is one of my favorite happy places. And it's the ultimate light and airy workspace, too.

PAGES 64–65: These curtains epitomize my minimalist approach to layering. PAGE 67: Location matters as much to fashion as to real estate, hence this Dior jacket in Palm Beach. PRECEDING OVERLEAF: We dedicated this apartment to art, and the art of design. Favorite pieces include Eric Schmitt's console and ceiling fixture; Jacques Garcia's occasional table; Vladimir Kagan's fabulous version tête-à-tête, and one of Josef Albers's *Homage to the Square* prints on a lighted easel from Lorin Marsh. RIGHT: Our almost all-white interior gets wonderful color from the views. Dedon's sculptural garden stool sits handily between Randolph & Hein lounge chairs dressed in a textured Schumacher woven. The sleek modern bench is from John Boone. OVERLEAF: George Williams's massive painting above a custom sofa from Anees Upholstery in a Holly Hunt fabric anchors the living room's second seating area. The desk and side table are by Kimberly Denman; the tray, by Hermès.

We wanted visiting family and friends to find the guest bedroom, which doubles as a work-from-home space, welcoming and cozy. Though I've never lived with pink, it almost made sense here. The mauve that anchors the room is my play on Palm Beach's classic pink-and-green combo and feels sophisticated with the room's chrome and anthracite accents. A sculptural chandelier adds energy in the center of the space. Antique mirrors over the leather headboard reflect light and make the space feel larger and brighter. Wool draperies with a graphic netting overlay add a touch of luxury.

ABOVE: This work area keeps things light with a custom desk from New Classics and Knoll's Saarinen chair in Zimmer + Rohde fabric beneath a commanding artwork by Victor Pasmore. OPPOSITE: MJ Atelier's custom wallpaper and Tech Lighting's mid-century glass globes make the entry a statement. The egg-shaped plaster sculpture by Thomas Pheasant creates a focal point at the end of the gallery.

Restrained tones in the dining area allow the forms to really speak. Comfortably elegant dining chairs from Troscan pull up to Knoll's iconic Saarinen table, which centers the space. Hervé van der Straeten's console adds function in a chic, sculptural way. Stone panels on the wall add to the textural mix.

The kitchen is a sweet spot for this cook, with Gaggenau appliances, onyx countertop by Cosentino, Rohl plumbing fixtures, and Downsview cabinetry. Phillip Jeffries's silver-leaf paper adds some shimmer. Dolomite Bianco marble pavers from Marmi Stone add nature's own pattern into the mix. The artwork is by Günther Förg.

ABOVE: Contrasting upholstery enhances the living room sofa. LEFT: Shine and reflection work moments of design magic. RIGHT: From the architecture to the art, the grid rules. BELOW: Zimmer + Rohde's grosgrain overlay superimposes its geometry onto curtain panels of a Carlton V wool.

ABOVE LEFT: Rubelli pillows
vary the grid. ABOVE RIGHT:
This dining room lamp is
from Pagani Studio.
LEFT: What's not to love
about lacquered drawer
interiors? BELOW LEFT: Eric
Schmitt's sleek console
serves its function fabulously.
BELOW RIGHT: A Janus et
Cie tray fits perfectly into
the material mix.

Cocooned in black, white, and grays, our primary bedroom is a cool, quiet retreat, especially when the curtains are drawn against the Florida sun. The play of textures and the bold, graphic art wake up the subdued palette with their energy. A Donald Judd work is suspended over the draperies in a fabric from Fret. The chairs are from Minotti.

I decided to go black, white, and graphic in the primary suite to let the art take center stage. The black ceiling that anchors the room makes the fan—a must in our tropical climate— disappear. The chairs at the foot of the bed balance the room.

One of the main reasons we purchased this home was the outdoor space. We furnished the balcony with seating areas that relate to their interior counterparts, and we separated the different areas with raffia dividers.

Our Palm Beach home is everything that we dreamed of, and that I designed for: a calming, serene environment where we can work, relax, and entertain, filled with the things we love.

ABOVE: An Alison Berger sconce, a Victoria + Albert sink, and Arte wallpaper animate the bath.
OPPOSITE: In an Armani for Rubelli fabric, the bed feels well tailored. A Ken Greenleaf series activates the bed wall. Zimmer + Rohde pillows and Frette bedding complete the suite.

The palette of the guest bedroom plays off Palm Beach's classic white and pink pairing with its pas de deux of Benjamin Moore's Simply White and Mauve. A ceiling fixture by Phoenix Day, Minotti side tables, pillows by Zimmer + Rhode, and Armani lamps bring the style and the substance. The art is by Ken Greenleaf (side wall), Jennifer Gibbs (on side table), and David Iatesta (above the bed). Let's just call this room an '80s throwback!

Richard Schultz's sleek, modern garden furnishings for Knoll have long been personal favorites—and they couldn't be better suited to outdoor living as we know it in Palm Beach. Woven of palmettos, the basket marks the spatial divider with texture and the craftsperson's touch.

ALL ABOUT ART

I've been fortunate on occasion to work with clients who are especially simpatico because we share the same passions. This Nashville homeowner has been one of those rare birds for me. She brought us in when she was mid-construction on her traditional center hall Colonial, and we designed her interiors to come as a surprise, given the way the home presents itself to the street. Here's why: Her life's passion is finding and supporting young artists. She also loves to entertain. We developed the rooms around her collections—art first and foremost, but also ceramics and couture clothing—and her tenacity, because she's always on the prowl for more.

With only so much space, and so much to fill it, we placed each artwork in elevation first, curating her collection while building multifunctional rooms to complement it. The two of us traveled to France for furnishings. We also refreshed some existing pieces to fold into the mix. As a result, this interior is clean, yet pristinely fussy in a detailed, deeply layered way. In other words, no ruffles, but lots of stuff.

We set the stage in the black, white, and gold entry hall with massed works from various artists, mostly from Maine, where the client has a summer home. She wanted to up the theatricality in the dining room across the way. I flew with my fabrics and paint swatches to Maine to develop the color scheme around a painting in the works. We dressed the walls in a handmade, gold leaf–flaked wall covering used in Chanel boutiques globally. With Murano glass-studded consoles, an ebonized dining table, and simple but boldly patterned curtain panels, this room makes any meal an occasion. A nearby guest room gave us a chance to change up the palette to chocolate, taupe, and white. It's different, but closely related, with wall covering that matches a rich chocolate leather headboard, and a modern chinoiserie side table that brings the ornament.

Lacquered tomato red and filled with favorite things, the library is warm and cozy. She didn't designate an artwork for this space, but Paris never fails. The voilà moments came when we found the large piece over the sofa in a Left Bank gallery and the 1940s-era Murano chandelier and resin table at a flea market.

PRECEDING OVERLEAF: In this art lover's entry hall, a brass console with shagreen inlays made by hand in Paris and a photograph by Joyce Tenneson create an opening statement. RIGHT: Myra Berg's spools launch the living room's color explosion and its complexity of curves. The rug by Frank Stella serves as the centerpiece; dressed in cotton velvet, a Vladimir Kagan sofa brings color into the room's core. Lee Broom's polished brass chandelier gleams overhead. Artwork by James Marshall focuses the fireplace wall. OVERLEAF LEFT: Charles Hollister's Lucite entry table adds function without blocking the view. The metal sculpture is by Laszlo Tompa. OVERLEAF RIGHT: The breakfast area opens off the living room and takes its color cues from the spools. Jeff Kellar's marble sculpture echoes the bench's channel-stitched upholstery.

The client's love of fashion inspired the formal dining room's black, white, and gold scheme. Hervé van der Straeten's fixture dangles like a statement earring from the gold-lacquered ceiling. A Joyce Tenneson photograph goes quietly with the color flow. OVERLEAF LEFT: Chicness on steroids, a wallcovering from Assemblage used in Chanel boutiques magically wraps the room; handmade in Arkansas, it features gold leaf on a thick painted ground. The client loves rock crystal; here, it brings its special glow to the consoles, mirrors, and table lamps that flank windows dressed in a boldly graphic Zimmer + Rohde fabric. OVERLEAF RIGHT: The butler's pantry, which displays the client's collection of Hermès china, and the wet bar glitter with antique mirror and rock crystal details. Oversized kitchen implements—sculptures found in Paris—bring the wit. Japanese paper light fixtures act to calm the glamour storm.

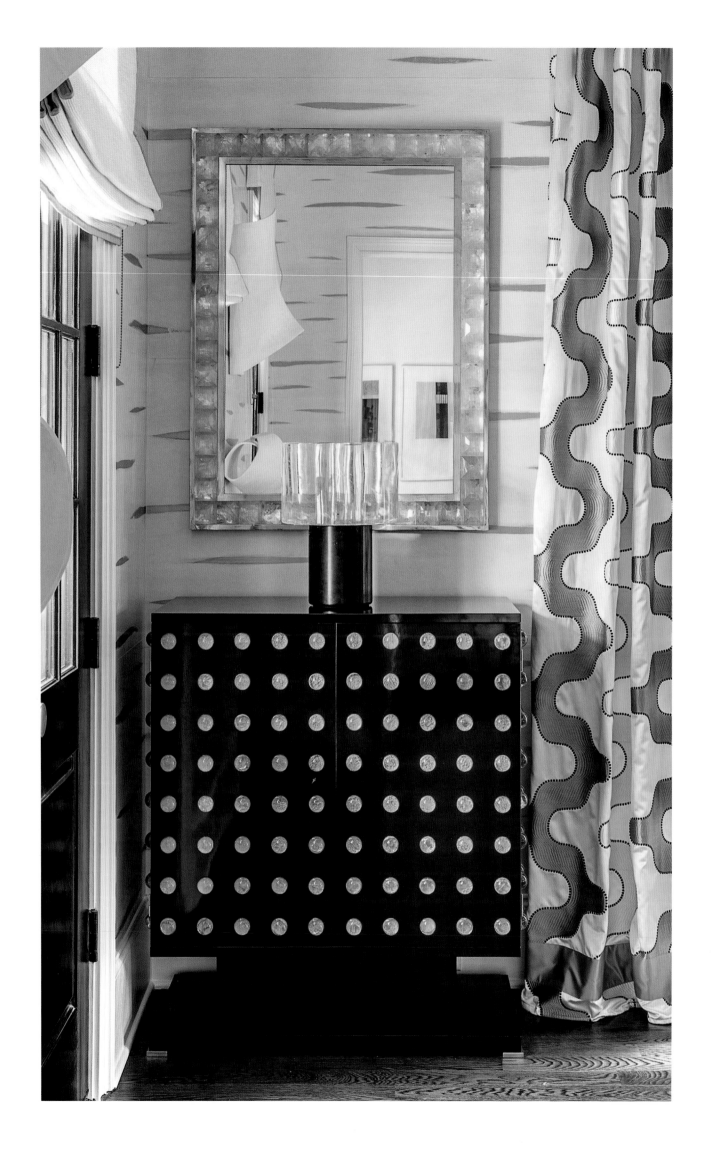

TOP LEFT: Gold rock crystal studs bejewel the lacquer consoles. TOP RIGHT: MJ Atelier's wallcovering adds dimension. ABOVE: A sculpture of paper bags adds a touch of humor. LEFT: With bold forms, colors, and textures, balance is key. RIGHT: For maximum visual impact, sometimes more is more.

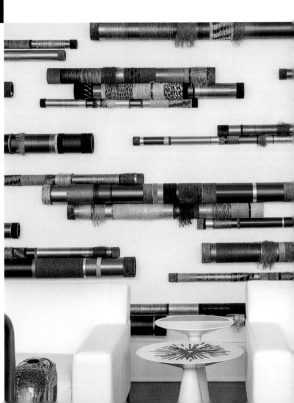

ABOVE: A hand-painted chinoiserie desk inserts an unexpected tracery detail in the guest bedroom. LEFT: An unusual rock crystal lamp with a hand-pleated sheer shade is just one of many fashion moments in her upstairs game room. BELOW: Plaster sculptures add even more movement to the dining room wall.

ABOVE: Chosen specifically to set off the artwork by J.T. Gibson, hand-applied Venetian plaster transformed this powder room into a jewel box. OPPOSITE: The lacquer walls that warm this library also complement the red-headed homeowner. With so much texture, the botanical print on the chair back and curtains adds a touch of pattern and a welcome nature reference. The vintage Murano fixture, found in Paris, came from a château on the French Riviera. OVERLEAF LEFT: Clear glass inserts in this stylish kitchen's upper cabinets create display cases for Murano art glass. OVERLEAF RIGHT: Antique mirror cabinet fronts tie the kitchen and wet bar together. A trio of Lee Brown pendants dangle sculpturally over the counter. Favorite everyday dishes bring colors of happiness.

An oversized, mohair-covered sectional brings the cozy to the upstairs game room drenched in a rich shade of teal and tailored with burgundy and terra-cotta accents. The curtains with their ombré effect were a first for me in terms of digital printing. The club chairs by Jonas Upholstery are covered in a painted art canvas. The custom mahjong table gets a regular workout. The moody painting that suggested the room's palette is by Jared Small.

The living room tells another art story. When she and I met, she had these fabulous spools of thread in her Memphis home and her retreat in Maine—the work of an artist on the West Coast. It took some convincing, but ultimately, she agreed that her living room needed them all—and more—so the artist came to create her installation. The carpet, a Frank Stella design, puts more art underfoot beneath iconic contemporary furnishings.

The kitchen we kept simple, with mirrored wood cabinets to match mirrored built-ins. The butler's pantry and bar carry more mirror between the dining room and kitchen. In the breakfast nook, bright color accents picked up from the thread-spool installation felt just right.

Her upstairs living room is her true go-to spot for mahjong games with friends—and it's our one exception from the gallery white envelope that prevails everywhere else. She gave me her hard-won dispensation here to color the walls in a dark, moody shade that we pulled from a favorite artwork. We then went full-on tonal with matching carpet, curtains, and a silk mohair-covered custom sectional. Which is not to say there is no sparkle, because sequined tape adorns the curtains' leading edges, though with great subtlety.

A series of seashell-encrusted dress forms made by a Maine artist in the manner of Christian Dior's "New Look" inspired her private suite of rooms, where we stuck as much as possible to furnishings by fashion designers who dabble in interior design. Hermès wallcovering swathes a bedroom converted to the perfect closet for her extensive collection of fine handbags. Her draped bedroom is glamour central with a Lucite bed that seems to float and artwork after artwork suspended from brass chains. A local faux painter and I went wild with the high ceiling and carried those colors into her sitting room. Her office plays off the teal of the living room, as does another guest bedroom.

This home celebrates art, and especially the art of life.

OPPOSITE: The wet bar with its built-ins couldn't be more convenient.
A collection of agate sculptures found in Paris bring a whisper of decoration
on high. The burgundy pinstripe adds definition to the cabinet fronts.

All the surfaces in the primary bedroom are special and luxurious. Silk drapes with pink banding wrap the space in a soft embrace. Decorative painter Darryl Garrison picked up and ran with the pinstripe detail overhead. Custom bedding from Edi B Fine Linens in London plays with the primary palette. The lighthearted chandelier is made of silk ribbon. The artwork between the windows is by Nancy Cheairs. OVERLEAF LEFT: The dressing room is so pretty and sophisticated in shades of taupe and blush. Walls covered in custom-colored paper from Hermès speak to the client's inner fashionista. The custom built-ins house her handbag and jewelry collections. A silk carpet from Stark casts light up from the floor. The dress form sculpture is by Brian White. OVERLEAF RIGHT: The tones of the dressing room thread through into the primary bedroom's sitting room. Hand-embroidered pillows from Holland & Sherry catch the eye with bracing pattern. The rock crystal coffee table is plastered with her collection of Herend figurines. The rug from Odegard, wallpaper from Zina Studios, and curtain banding resonate with the primary bedroom's palette. PAGE 114: The primary bath repeats the Hermès wallpaper. The corset sculpture is by Brian White. PAGE 115: We selected the marble with large figuring so as not to compete with the wallpaper.

ABOVE: With its red ceiling, walls wrapped in a custom botanical by MJ Atelier, leather-topped Hermès desk, and luxe chaise by Dmitriy & Co., the client's office is serene at heart but filled with energy, which suits her to a T. OPPOSITE: Billy Baldwin poufs and a vintage J. Robert Scott console with a white-gold hand-painted frieze and matching mirror reflect her love of great American decoration. An Hermès Kelly bag memorialized in resin takes pride of place on the console top.

The patio is as richly layered with art, accessories, and details as any of the indoor rooms. The outdoor fireplace creates a quotient of cozy. Seating from Amalfi arranged around the hearth features cushions in performance fabrics colored to tie into the garden beyond; the espaliered Kieffer pears climbing the fence reverse that balance of green and white. The floor lamps are from Kettal.

CONTEMPORARY LONDON LIVING

Every family we work with has their own sensibility, taste, and comfort level with decoration. For some, more is more. Others prefer a happy middle ground of not too much/not too little. These design-loving, Europe-based clients are strict minimalists. They believe that less is more. And they live it, as their four-bedroom, four-story London home—a new property built on an old mindset, with architecture that's quite stark compared to a more traditional rowhouse—shows clearly. What's interesting, though, is that the strict aesthetic doesn't translate into the absence of decoration. It just puts greater pressure on every choice. Furnishings in minimalist environments behave almost like objects, so each individual piece needs to have a powerful enough visual presence to command the space, while the mix has to work as a force multiplier for balance, harmony, and impact.

This home's open-plan, railroad-style ground floor axial layout adds to the challenge. The entry steps directly into the dining area, which opens to the kitchen, which unfolds to the living room and outdoor space. In other words, the whole of the home's public-facing zone is visible at a glance. This means we had to find ways to differentiate individual areas that, paradoxically, also created overall cohesion.

These clients love the classicism of black and white, and the streamlined effect of built-in storage. They have a thing for the play of textures and finishes—beautiful stone, rich woods, lacquer finishes, luxurious fabrics, and polished metals—infused with jolts of bold color, in moderation, and art. These are the tools we used to bring this interior to life.

In the dining room, the glossy contrasts with the matte, leather softens marble and wood, curves resonate against straight lines. The built-in unit, which we repeated in the kitchen zone, serves as both storage and bar with a very mid-century, Florence Knoll-inspired vibe. A series of framed, contemporary prints and the Murano chandelier—think Capiz shells, but in glass, in technicolor—lighten the look here.

PRECEDING OVERLEAF: Shades of gray with a pop of color create an interesting, stylish conversation area within this family room. The mid-century sculpture by Curtis Jeré practically takes flight off the coffee table. The botanical charcoal brings a reference to the garden inside. Eric Schmitt's vase extends their collection of fine glass. RIGHT: Shelves filled with art books are accessorized in the clear, minimalist fashion that resonates with this young family in London. A play of textures adds to the room's energy. Sheers that filter the light add a gauzy softness. The laser-cut leather side table is from Poltrona Frau. The chaises are covered in cowhide.

The dining room at the front of the house sets the interior's classic mid-century modernist tone. The chandelier from Vistosi adds vivaciousness and speaks naturally to the series of Joan Miró prints that take center stage above built-in storage inspired by the designs of Florence Knoll. The pair of ghostly lamps from Vistosi subtly insert some contrasting forms into the mix.

The kitchen is not just a workspace and gathering place. It's also the transition zone between the front and back of the house. Sleek, modern, and all-white, it's something of a visual palette cleanser. To make things more interesting, we added a wall of high-gloss aubergine lacquered panels to hide the pantry, a very sculptural island lit by a pair of fabulous pendant lights that bring the contrasting geometry, and an installation of Fornasetti plates for graphic spice.

We made the most of every square inch, or rather, centimeter, from the front to the back, and especially in the living area. Creating a floor-to-ceiling storage wall opposite the fireplace served two purposes. It provided a natural place to switch out the materials and create ample space for the clients' library. We used texture to make a cool, sexy, modern statement with hide, laser-cut leather, wool, and lacquer, and kept the palette comparatively neutral, though we used darker gray tones for contrast and as a comment on London's general weather. A sectional sofa anchors the cozy seating area, supplemented by a leather, nesting coffee table, laser-cut leather stools, and a pair of low-slung, wire-framed chairs. Pillows inject notes of bright color that are easy to switch out. As in the dining room, gauze sheers soften the lines of the architecture, and the boundary between indoors and outdoors. The adjoining furnished terrace—large by any urban standards, and quite unusual in London because of the rain—extends our graphic black-and-white motif into the richly textured environment of brick and concrete.

Upstairs is their primary suite. Here, we brought the luxe with gilded and leafed moments, inviting textures, touches of surprise, and a serene palette that harmonizes warm and cool tones just beautifully. A few choice bolts of red as well as a pair of Picasso prints keeps the space from being too quiet.

Here's to the minimalist aesthetic, especially when it's not so minimalist after all.

This family loves and collects fine glass. The pantry's eggplant lacquer doors complement the Murano pieces that thread through the house and heighten the profile of the casual dining area's sculptural chairs.

All in white, the kitchen and casual dining zone provides a high-functioning transition space between two areas rich in color. We chose the deep purple from Fine Paints of Europe for its high visual impact and reference to royalty. A trio of glass fixtures hovers over the long island, continuing the circle-meets-square motif.

LEFT: Light flows uninterrupted through this interior.
RIGHT: A Murano mirror and Pierre Frey wallpaper turn the powder room into an art installation. BELOW: Nashville-based English artist Ed Nash, this work's creator, reflects the family's both-sides-of-the-pond heritage. BOTTOM LEFT: A Picasso lithograph brings art close. BOTTOM RIGHT: The entry feels like the English countryside.

RIGHT: Both nightstands offer an intimate moment with Picasso. BELOW LEFT: The vanity chair inserts a crimson pop into this serene sleeping space with European-style built-in oak cabinetry. BELOW RIGHT: A fur inset brings a touch of the unexpected to the bench at the foot of the bed. BOTTOM RIGHT: Textured gold leaf transforms the bed wall.

ABOVE: We designed the custom headboard to mimic the baseline of the Phillip Jeffries wallpaper with its gold-leaf sky; the upholstery fabric creates an ombré effect with the wall, while the charcoal stripe adds dimension. The nightstands with lacquered asymmetrical drawers are from Talisman; their sculptured fronts are finished in 14-carat yellow gold leaf.
OPPOSITE: The exterior brickwork and gray London sky inspired the interior palette.

ABOVE: Pattern can work wonders in spaces small and large. In the tight confines of this powder room, it is vibrant and transformative. OPPOSITE: In the garden, all the color comes from nature. The woven settee accentuates the dark window frames; the upholstery is from Sunbrella. The leopard-print pillows subtly bring pattern into a world of no pattern.

MY MODERN MIX

When you know, you know. That's how it is for me with houses, including our home in Nashville. We'd been looking for months and were on holiday in Bali when a good friend emailed an alert that this house, built in the late 1970s and designed by the Chicago-based style maven Richard Himmel, was coming on the market. I knew it would sell before we got home, so, although neither of us had ever stepped foot inside, we submitted an offer from the Singapore Airport as we were waiting for a connecting flight back to the U.S. Thirty hours later, we landed in Nashville, got in the car, went see it, and fell in love in real life.

The house we found was a fantastic architectural envelope with an open floor plan, interesting surviving original details, an extended outdoor terrace, white walls, and a flat roof that nodded to mid-century Palm Springs. That said, it had been altered unsympathetically—each wall was a different Easter egg color, trimmed in chocolate brown. So, it was everything we'd been looking for: contemporary, yet with many classical elements, great for entertaining, and with the need to be transformed.

We never looked back. The local company that had shaped and carved the house's original mill-work in 1978 still had all the knives they'd used then, so we were able to restore the interiors to what they would have been with authentic architectural detail. We also created a bar in the living room, updated the kitchen and baths, and replaced the windows and doors throughout.

The original, embossed aluminum double front doors set the tone for our private world behind the façade. The double-height foyer unfolds into a huge living room with its original eighteen-foot ceilings and terrazzo flooring intact. We didn't have a single piece of furniture that fit its grand scale. But I'd always wanted to design a room around a piano, so we started with that until the rest of our furniture arrived. My goal was to create a living room/library with clean, simple but interesting pieces. I decided to create an island for living in the room's core, arranging a large sectional sofa with built-in bookshelves, two oversized club chairs, and a pair of Jean-Michel Frank swivel chairs dressed in blue velvet around a four-foot-square coffee table. The cascading wool sheers that drape the double-height glass doors to the terrace are my touch of the romantic.

PAGE 137: The entry sets the tone for all that follows. Our stamped aluminum front doors with their double "C" handles are original to the house, as is the vintage millwork. The coat cabinet fronted with Hermès suede introduces a soft texture into the material mélange. RIGHT: Our double-height living room is the heart of our home. Here, silk velvet–upholstered lounge chairs and ottoman from Mattaliano, which pick up on the piano's curves, introduce a pop of color into the otherwise neutral environment; contrast welting sharpens the outlines, bringing the forms into focus with the blockier geometries. The oversized-check throw from Prada adds another comment into the play of scale and proportion.

ABOVE: Karl Springer's hand sculpture, made as a gift for Albert Hadley, is an everyday reminder of two of my design heroes. The upholstery fabric on our Armani Casa armchairs reflects the room's motifs in miniature. OPPOSITE: This overhead view reveals the play of shapes clearly. Dark carpet grounds the room's composition in the white space.

The dining area centers on my custom, bird's-eye maple–topped table, now called the Savage Table in Keith Fritz's line. The leather-upholstered chairs are lean, elegant, and very comfortable. Jamie Drake's chandelier for Boyd Lighting adds shine and a touch of shagreen overhead. For energy and visual interest, I carefully curated the wall of black-and-white accessories with favorite pieces.

We planned to use the dining area as a dining/library space, so I made sure to include a built-in shelving system for storage and reconfigure the adjacent kitchen with an island. The dining table is my own design. Handmade in Indiana by Keith Fritz (and still in his collection), it features a bleached, bird's-eye maple top outlined in black lacquer that complements our new kitchen cabinets.

The primary suite on the other side of the living room is an oasis, filled with our favorite pieces from favorite places. I chose the black, white, and chartreuse palette not just because I love it and it makes sense here, but also so I could play with the graphic power of positive and negative space, literally and figuratively. The volcanic black Venetian plaster that finishes the bed wall introduces a special sheen that sets off the leather bed and makes the TV on the side wall disappear. The seating area adds not just more comfort, but function, too. It's a great spot to cozy up with the computer and get things done.

A spiral staircase climbs to a catwalk that connects the upstairs bedrooms and bath. We converted one of the bedrooms to a home office with a Jacques Adnet-inspired leather desk, chairs originally from the private client room at Van Cleef & Arpels' New York boutique, sheer cashmere window panels, and artworks by local artists.

This house has been great for entertaining in all seasons. And we live outdoors when we can, thanks to our terrace, which is grill area, dining space, and lounge all in one.

Here's to love at first sight.

The graphic pattern of this Zimmer + Rohde's fabric creates a wonderful backdrop for the room, setting off the neutral palette and encouraging the forms of the sculpture and lines of the pedestal to really stand out. The table is set with our Ginori china.

Bird's-eye maple serves like connective tissue, gathering the dining room and kitchen into a cohesive unit. Black lacquer pinstripes and leather-wrapped pulls add defining accents to the geometry of the cabinet fronts. My Shatter wallpaper for Carleton V speaks to the room's various lines, including the applied-leather stripes on the Roman shade over the sink. Black granite countertops are a favorite work surface.

LEFT: Curves and cubes in small scale create a fascinating visual dialogue. RIGHT: The art complements the stairwell's verticality. BELOW: An Armani Casa screen enhances the living room's graphic drama. BOTTOM LEFT: A Cartier ruler brings shine to a ceramic tabletop. BOTTOM RIGHT: The Fornasetti bedside table pops against the dark wall.

TOP: Patent leather sets off the bar's Schott Zwiesel glassware and Waterworks sink. ABOVE LEFT: Melissa Turner's sinuous ceramic sculpture enhances the mix of forms. ABOVE RIGHT: An Hermès lacquer tray in acid yellow is unmissable in the visual landscape. LEFT: A limewashed desk and chair in Hermès leather add to the guest room's hospitality.

Our home office vies for "chicest room in the house" honors. The cerulean leather–topped, Jacques Adnet–style desk, matching silk velvet–covered sofa, and Hermès wallpaper with a bridle motif give the room a serious masculine vibe. The ceramic garden stool—a perfect drinks table—chats with the room's other striped elements.

Artie loves to get cozy on the woven fur throw at the foot of our bed. Venetian plaster walls cocoon the room in a dark embrace that's just perfect for working and sleeping. The Italian pendant mirror that adds a touch of irony is poised like a pediment above our leather-channeled headboard. The bedding is Frette's Liquid Silver. The curtain fabric and bolster are from Jack Lenor Larsen.

The bedroom's seating area ups the ante with its play on stripes and Joseph Guay's feather-light photograph. The leather-upholstered, skirted ottoman does double duty as an occasional table. The skull pillow from Alexander McQueen is a true fashion moment. OVERLEAF: We love to entertain and set up our patio with an outdoor kitchen for that purpose. The grilling area furnishings are from Janus et Cie; in black with contrasting piping, they tie into each of the surrounding rooms. Boxwood parterres add greenery. A Murano glass sculpture draws all eyes to the coffee table. The superhero is from Vondom.

PATTERN PLAY WITH A PURPOSE

I'm a great believer in the idea that there are principles and guidelines for successful interiors, but not hard-and-fast rules. With second homes like this one for longtime clients in Rosemary Beach, Florida, I have a modus operandi. For every home away from home, comfort comes first so everyone can relax. And no matter how sophisticated the clients want their furnishings to be, the rooms have to be multifunctional for practicality. My fabric choices tend to celebrate the indoor/outdoor options because they support the vacation-home lifestyle, and with multiple generations usually present, we want to safeguard everything from sand to small sticky fingers.

When this couple, recent empty nesters with three daughters living in other states, asked for my help in creating this home as their getaway place and as a second homestead for family and friends, I had the decision-making framework clear in my mind. Rubbed linens and wipeable performance fabrics were perfect for the monochromatic feel they wanted. Here and there in the public spaces, we slipped in moments of a soft, elegant blue, like the water and sky at the beach, and true pops of color in the more private ones. We choreographed the elements of the interior to evolve into a seamlessly woven thread starting at the front door. With Venetian plaster walls, sandy limestone floors, and artwork from artists throughout the South, the combination was a perfect fit for the environment in which the house stands.

The house sits on a capacious corner lot with a vast backyard entertaining space that unfolds from a large, truly gracious loggia with expansive living and dining areas and a fully equipped kitchen out onto the neighborhood's largest pool, set into a beautifully manicured landscape of lawn and gardens.

A private wing with the primary suite occupies one end of the home. The other end is devoted to the interior's public zone for entertaining, with well-appointed dining, living, and connecting spaces. The home's many happy features include an intimate breakfast nook, a chef's kitchen with a large scullery attached, two guest rooms on the main level, two more upstairs, plus two bunk rooms—one tucked under the eaves, another positioned conveniently off the back entry—plus another guest house above the garage. There's also a comfortable in-home theater that's a perfect hanging-out space for everyone to watch sports and movies together. Yet the house was built without a proper dining room, so we co-opted the oval-shaped entry for that purpose with a spectacular, dual-purpose bronze center hall table that sets the tone for the entire house.

PAGE 158: Knoxville Gray from Benjamin Moore brings a touch of home to this Rosemary Beach, Florida, house by architect Lew Oliver. PRECEDING OVERLEAF LEFT: The front door opens directly to the impactful foyer–dining room. The lanterns are by Bevolo Lighting. PRECEDING OVERLEAF RIGHT: Venetian plaster walls give this connecting hallway a special glow. Poufs of woven burlap layer texture on texture. ABOVE: Beadboard walls feel right at the back entry. The woven wicker console adds another rustic texture, which contrasts beautifully with the Swedish side chair. The hand-painted ceramic is a Paris find. The painting is by McKenzie Dove. OPPOSITE: In the entry hall–dining room, curtain panels from Pierre Frey complement the swaying palms outdoors. Tropical-style rattan chairs from McGuire are upholstered in performance fabric for easy maintenance. The Jean de Merry table fits naturally into the oval-shaped room; the transparency of its glass top keeps things light in the room's core. The chandelier is from John Boone.

The living room is all casual elegance with its play of textures and pattern. A sculptural console divides the room into two distinct seating areas. Dressed in a soft chenille, the four upholstered armchairs from Ferrell Mittman couldn't be more inviting, especially gathered around the vinyl-covered ottoman. Woven curtain panels from Fret introduce a smallish-scale pattern that speaks directly to the burlap poufs. Handcrafted faux bois ceramics by Roy Hamilton provide a reference to nature. Silver-leafed sconces from Apparatus add notes of sheen. Paper-backed silk fabric in the niche helps carry pattern around the room.

ABOVE: The living area flows organically into both the kitchen and an adjacent reading nook made cozy with a fireplace. The oversized stainless-steel hood works decoratively like a piece of modern sculpture. Fixtures from Apparatus over the island help create cohesion. OPPOSITE: Woven rattan bar stools from Palecek thread another texture into the composition. The scullery opens conveniently off the kitchen.

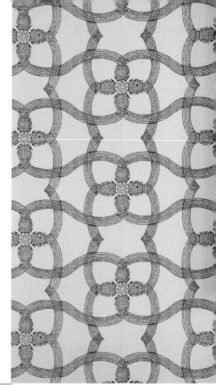

ABOVE LEFT: Neutrals and textures can create a spa-like environment. ABOVE RIGHT: Muriel Brandolini custom-colored silk upholsters the niche wall. RIGHT: Teak balls turn the fireplace into a sculpture garden. BELOW LEFT: Japanese paper shows the beauty of the handmade. BELOW RIGHT: Ship rigging inspired the bunkroom's rope detail.

TOP: A Gregorius Pineo table layers in more texture. ABOVE LEFT: Carolyn Carr's artwork sings above a vintage wicker trunk; the indoor-outdoor rug continues the blue motif. ABOVE RIGHT: Scullery shelves house tableware plus objects found in area antiquing. LEFT: A Liaigre sofa is great for curling up with a book.

The couple wanted a departure from their traditional primary residence in Nashville, so we chose classic contemporary furnishings with beautiful, clean lines and, occasionally, a slightly edgy attitude. White is so cooling in tropical surroundings that we decided to let it predominate here, then we played up the textures and added tones inspired by the pickled pecky cypress accents that fan throughout the house. The result is clean, crisp, and stylishly casual.

The family room was large enough for three seating groups: one with banquettes flanking a fireplace; one with a cluster of four swivel chairs near the kitchen; and one with a sofa and a pair of occasional chairs near the entry hall/dining area. Custom wallcoverings—one, for example, is little fish—add graphic impact on selected walls for energy. Slightly rustic raw silk pillows and sisal carpets on the limestone floors add layers of depth and texture.

Textured grass cloth wraps the walls of the primary suite, with a fabulous graphic fabric and luxurious bedding for balance. The main guest quarters feature spa-like textures with occasion punches of color and pattern. Upstairs under the eaves, the bunk room in full-on nautical mode—smart stripes, pops of red woodwork, and jib-like sail dividers between the built-ins—gives the guests a fun hideaway. The ground-floor bunk room is more understated, yet no less fresh thanks to its primarily white look sparked with pops of sunshine yellow.

The covered spaces of the entertaining loggia—full kitchen, relaxed living room, and open-air dining areas—connect seamlessly to the interior rooms with teak furnishings that carry this home's welcome-to-transitional-coastal-living aesthetic out of doors.

Neutral but textured, layered but simple, livable and functional, this home feels fresh with performance fabrics, graphic art, patterned wall coverings, art, and accessories—just the right mix for this family, at the beach, today.

OPPOSITE: Pecky cypress paneling gives the breakfast a warm, snug feel. The chrome and high-gloss table is also great for cards. OVERLEAF LEFT: Lily pad wallpaper in the guest bath picks up the palette of the guest room next door. OVERLEAF RIGHT: A work by local artist Tess Davies focuses the guest room's bed wall. A coral-like fabric from Liberty upholsters the bed.

A custom-colored stripe from Christopher Farr sets the nautical tone for this bunkroom that sleeps six. The sail-inspired dividers are rigged with woven cotton rope. Zinc lanterns with antique glass insets that recall running lights add another flourish to the shipboard theme.

ABOVE: The upstairs playroom is fresh and fun in shades of blue and white used in a very modern way. All the upholstered pieces are covered in wipeable, cleanable performance fabric for easy everyday maintenance. OPPOSITE: Art adds spots of brilliant color around the foosball table.

ABOVE: Kentucky bluestone, teak, and pecky cypress overhead give this indoor-outdoor dining area its distinctive spirit. The lanterns are from Bevolo Lighting. OPPOSITE: A covered seating area behind the pool offers relief from the sun when desired. The bentwood lounge chairs are incredibly comfortable and great for wet bathing suits. Woven palmetto leaves couldn't be more local; they flank the opening that overlooks the back lawn.

178

With parterres of lawn and paving and carefully positioned palms that rise like columns, symmetry creates comfort at this poolside. Rich teal accenting the architectural details makes reference to the local flora. The chairs on the pool ledge are covered in a performance fabric from Perennials.

MUSIC CITY MINIMALISM

Minimalist design in my view is really the most interesting kind of double dare. It demands extreme visual discipline and ultimate precision in the execution. Each decision, detail, form, shape, material, object, relationship, you name it, needs to be as close to perfection for the specific clients and spaces as possible because everything, but everything, shows. What's not to love about that? Transforming the less-is-more ethos into luxurious, more-with-less interiors was the task this British family of four presented with their Nashville home, designed by a local architectural firm with both Greek and Asian influences. The parents are serious design aficionados, and their daughters are instilled in the world of design, also. The entire family has a passion for powerful, stripped-down minimalist architecture—and for decorating, too, as long as it's in the same luxe, highly selective, pared back-to-the-most-elegant-essentials mode and spirit. And they truly love spaces that are all about air, light, form, volume, comfort, and the art of restraint.

From the front door to the poolside, in areas both public and private, we designed this home to be at one with the architecture from the moment of entry, which plays with the effects of compression and expansion. In the entry hall, a large black-and-white photograph dominates the stair wall. Past this tightly contained foyer, a sleek wall of built-in storage leads down one step to the dining area proper. Along a side wall, a gloss lacquer, Asian-inspired console topped by a beveled mirror hints at the gist of the colors, shapes, and materials palette to come. At the core, a marble oval-topped table rests on a quadrilinear brass base, setting up the push-and-pull of line meeting curve that we used to bring an energizing tension to these spare spaces. A suite of taupe leather dining chairs folds another luxe material into the mix, as well as a warm hue that tempers the basic black-and-white scene.

Another step descends to the open-plan living area, which unfolds into the light thanks to the wall of sliding glass doors that runs the entire width of the house and connects this Paris-inspired, loft-like, multifunction space to the poolside. We wanted this expanse to flow organically. The kitchen and breakfast area center on Warren Platner's classic, modern, wire-based table embraced by French designer Hugues Chevalier's chairs, all beneath Southern fine artist Joseph Guay's quietly spectacular Selenite disk (60 inches in circumference) embedded with gold flakes for just the right note

PRECEDING OVERLEAF: The entry is all about levels of sheen, high gloss, and reflection with the polished concrete floor, lacquer console, carefully curated selection of objects, and mirror. The graphic sheers provide privacy. RIGHT: In this less-is-more interior, we strictly edited the pieces because with simplicity, everything shows. The web-backed chairs in the living room's primary seating area are from B&B Italia; the laser-cut screen, which adds both lightness and privacy, is from Poltrona Frau. Sheers wrap this space like a scrim and soften the architecture in an appropriately minimalist idiom.

The living room's second seating area is more intimate, set up for conversation à deux or for reading. The transition from the area rug to the blond oak flooring to the polished concrete underfoot sets the baseline of the palette and our response in terms of forms and textures. The kitchen millwork blends into the walls; the fridge complements the German window sashes. OVERLEAF LEFT: The breakfast area's brass-based Warren Platner table and spectacular Joseph Guay sculpture bring sparkle with warmth into this all-white world. The chairs are by Hugues Chevalier. OVERLEAF RIGHT: Lee Broom's pendant fixtures insert pinpoints of black into the overhead space to tie the area together. The sculpture at the window echoes the geometry all around it.

of glamor. This area flows into an intimate seating area à deux for reading and hanging out on the other side of the kitchen island and then to a conversation area. To mark this terminal wall decoratively (and balance the bling), we opted for a modern take on a traditional multipaneled screen with a fretwork-style, laser-cut leather screen in front of the window. A cascade of gauze sheers sheathe the window wall, yet veil the living space with barely-there, yet-impactful softness and a breath of romance.

For the primary suite upstairs, this couple wanted more of a luxe cocoon than an austere retreat. To that end, we used wheat and cream tones, an array of plush textures, and hints of brass accents to infuse the room with warmth. The carpet sets the stage with just a hint of pattern. The basic black furnishings add gravity. The pillows work the visual power of geometry. And the art brings the illusion of motion that adds some real drama.

This home suits this couple's personality to a T. And although it was a challenge, I feel like we captured beautifully how they wish to live. Because of their level of discernment and determined pursuit of modern perfection, for them the objects must always be the central focal point, which means the rooms become the ultimate display background—the velvet for the jewelry, as it were—that allows the individual pieces of furniture, accessories, and art to glory in the spotlight.

In the highly disciplined décor of the dining room, a decorative light fixture was unnecessary. Leather-wrapped Italian dining chairs bring tailored comfort to the table with its sculptural metal base and sleek polished top.

TOP LEFT: The screen influenced the sofa fabric from Designers Guild. TOP RIGHT: The bookstand is functional sculpture. ABOVE LEFT: Decorative cohesion matters in an open plan. ABOVE RIGHT: The candlesticks visually connect the table and wall sculpture. RIGHT: The webbing adds another neutral to the palette.

LEFT: Slab marble accents the front door. BELOW: In the primary bedroom, the palette widens to include champagne. BOTTOM LEFT: A pop of blue in the bath's white space feels fresh, bright, and cheery. BOTTOM RIGHT: The architecture's geometry and materiality were the design drivers here.

ABOVE: In the primary bath, marble slabs create a backdrop that accentuates the tub and presents it as the room's centerpiece. OPPOSITE: With the minimalist palette extending to the poolside, this house demonstrates indoor-outdoor living at its finest.

VILLA WESTVIEW

Have you ever imagined living in an Italian villa? Or designing one? Few people who admire this type of architecture and design also have the determination and persistence that it takes to build one. This couple, inspired by a love affair with architecture and Italy, did exactly that in the heart of Nashville's Belle Meade neighborhood with architect Ron Farris and interior architect and designer Jerry Begley, completing construction in 2009.

My first design encounter with these two came some years after the house was completed, when they brought me in to address an issue with the library's lacquered walls, which we solved by upholstering them in leather panels. Years later, they asked me to contemporize the rooms—soaring, beautifully proportioned, operatically decorated, and period-inspired—to look more modern. We decided to wield the power of paint, for starters, opting for a lighter palette to replace the existing Pompeiian hues and allow the marble accents and fabulous laser-cut floors to take the lead in color and pattern. For two years, our decorative painters worked their magic in finishes from lacquer to Venetian plaster on the home's practically palatial level of ornament and detail, everything from moldings, coffered ceilings, and paneled walls to built-in storage, chair and picture rails, wainscoting, and so much more.

One thing led to another, as often happens in the game of dominoes that is design. To suit the reimagined spaces we pulled in furnishings, antiques, and objects from the family's various other houses, which we reupholstered, refinished, re-envisioned, and rearranged. The exterior rooms received a similar top-to-bottom makeover to make sure the inside and outside breathed as one. Finally, we rehung art, both existing and new pieces, to put the finishing touches on the process of endowing this home with fresh life.

In the grand salon—the very formal living room—we updated the upholstered walls, replacing the oh-so-centuries-ago-style damask with a smart, crisp performance fabric. Next, we lightened almost everything in the furniture department, assembling a mix of Jean-Michel Frank chairs, ultra-luxe, classic modern sofas, Italian side chairs, and a mahogany console to form the spine of the room's back-to-back seating groups. The art deco influences, gilded antique Italian chairs upholstered in a fresh fabric and framed by a new Persian rug with classic motifs and soft hues, layer the modern look on a traditional base of expected pattern with updated colors—so twenty-first-century formal.

Freshly wallpapered, the dining room echoes this same chic, comfortable spirit of living with history, rather than in it. A fabulous long table can seat fourteen beneath a pair of contemporary chandeliers fabricated from antique parts. Undressed windows along the courtyard wall feel very up to date and connect the indoors and outside seamlessly. High-backed dining chairs add bracing notes of turquoise leather, kept in check by the silk fabric on the chair backs.

The library was cocooned in deep ebony for contrast with the faux leather walls. The Greek key of the room's marquetry trim established a pattern language we couldn't help but expand on with corresponding carpet, pillows, and curtains in varying scales. As ancient as this pattern is, it shouts MODERN in its bold, unfussy geometry.

The kitchen–breakfast room, family room, office, and guest bedrooms all received, in addition to a fresh coat (or ten) of paint, a lot of design love, be it new barstools and sofas, new carpets and lighting, repurposed draperies, a glamorous sheath of reflective, custom-painted wallpaper, or reupholstered headboards.

Similar reprogramming happened upstairs in the primary guest suite, where we adopted more pieces from their various homes and rehung the chandelier draperies formerly in the dining room (the two rooms have the same dimensions). Both the husband's and wife's offices received updates. Hers began with fresh wallpaper; his, with lacquered walls and repurposed drapery in a Fortuny patterned fabric to fold in a reminder of Venice.

Viva Italia. And Nashville too!

PRECEDING OVERLEAF: In recasting this Italian-inspired villa in Nashville for today's lifestyle, less became more. Repainting the entry foyer allowed the architecture to speak; the addition of Dali's portrait of Lincoln helped set the new tone. ABOVE AND OPPOSITE: In creating their home, this family valued verisimilitude.

PRECEDING OVERLEAF: There's always comfort in symmetry. Beyond the paint magic, taking the grand salon from formal to casual involved establishing a pair of seating groups with shared design DNA to make the room more usable and inviting. Switching out the art from classic to modern and pulling together a mix of furnishings from different periods also helped make the space feel more contemporary; the chandeliers, candle sconces, and art deco console were holdovers. RIGHT: Mohair upholstery added luxurious texture. Tones of blue thread throughout this interior, as do tones of green, here in the malachite obelisks.

The absence of drapes in the dining room let the architecture come to the fore. Shagreen wallcovering from Schumacher created a deco vibe in a completely contemporary way. Leather chairs from Dennis and Leen added pleasing moments of saturated color. The table is set for a party with flowers from the garden just beyond the French doors. OVERLEAF: In the library, we recast classic into modern classic with leather walls, black lacquer details and trim, antiques, and a vivid Greek key motif. Leather-trimmed Hermès drapes, a pair of chairs from Maison Jansen in velvet tweed, and deco-inspired club chairs in channeled velvet layered in luxurious textures.

Fresh paint and a new stone slab on the island gave the existing kitchen a much lighter look, one in keeping with today's lifestyle.

Repainting the breakfast room worked wonders to bring it into today's lighter aesthetic. Reupholstered seating took cues from the floor's terra-cotta tones. The long, shiny refectory table, which seats eight to ten, centered the arrangement under the existing chandelier. The recarpeted stairs carried the motif of blues to the second floor.

ABOVE: The primary bedroom provided an opportunity to play with ideas of modern glamour. Reupoholstering the walls in damask imbued the space with a refinement that, while resonant of history, felt completely current. We refreshed the mix of existing furnishings with pieces from the clients' other properties, including a chest from their California home. OPPOSITE: Lacquered in Benjamin Moore Aegean Olive under a white chocolate ceiling, the husband's office recalls the Mediterranean region that inspired them to build the house. Rearranged art, a new coffee table, and drapes reused from another location enhance this sensibility.

212

ABOVE LEFT: The guest bath became a bower with de Gournay paper. ABOVE RIGHT: Painted scrollwork in the primary bath recalls Italy. RIGHT: Greek key trim tied his office and bath together. BELOW LEFT: New wallpaper updated the pool bath. BELOW RIGHT: Venetian plaster lightened this powder room.

ABOVE LEFT: Rich pattern and color enliven this guest bath. ABOVE RIGHT AND BELOW RIGHT: Gracie paper transformed the main-floor powder's two rooms. LEFT: The primary's stone-set bath and glass-encased shower. RIGHT AND BELOW LEFT: Repainted, the primary bath merges ancient and modern into timeless.

PRECEDING OVERLEAF LEFT: Turning the hall to the wine cellar into a gallery was a natural decision. Adding a carpet helped finish the space with a flourish. PRECEDING OVERLEAF RIGHT: Handcrafted millwork enhanced the wine cellar. RIGHT: New upholstery, carefully curated contemporary art, a TV cabinet, and a contemporary fireplace screen turned the keeping room off the kitchen into a much-loved, much-used everyday space. The upholstery on the swivel chairs is from Osborne & Little.

ABOVE: Janus et Cie teak furnishings chosen to complement the wood ceiling give a cohesiveness to the outdoor dining pavilion. The pizza oven makes this space a special favorite. OPPOSITE: Michael Taylor's classic outdoor furnishings in shades from nature bring modern comfort to the terrace off the grand salon that overlooks the pool. OVERLEAF: Classic modern pieces from Brown Jordan Furniture recast the poolside areas for today's lifestyle.

SHOW HOUSE DREAMS

Show houses are my dream factories, and my laboratory, too. Each one I've participated in has presented me with an unparalleled opportunity to explore ideas that have been percolating in the studio, to put my creativity to the test in the moment, and to understand how my personal aesthetic is evolving, and that of my colleagues and the industry as well. But best of all for me, every show house benefits a good cause, so they give me a chance to give back, too.

My first show house, in 2013, was to benefit my alma mater, O'More College of Architecture and Design at Belmont University in Nashville. O'More subsequently mounted show houses in 2014, 2016, and 2017. Each allowed me to spread my decorating wings further. The first year, I dressed a tiny breakfast room in a graphic style with furnishings that I loved at the time and felt that people needed to see. Mostly, I used this room to pay homage to the late Herbert Rodgers, the old-school Nashville decorator who gave Albert Hadley his start. The following year, our venue was a Victorian house, a former funeral home, and I had the opportunity to show off my furniture design skills in the enormous entry with a center hall table that is in the maker's collection to this day. Because the moldings were outstanding, I added more, painted them all white to make the details pop, and played up the confection with warm charcoal walls—traditional enough for the period of the house, yet still clean, elegant, and unfussy. In 2016, for a home office on the second floor, I went blue, and shifted the mode into a more contemporary spirit. The color story held the following year in the formal dining room, beefed up with gold, made glamorous with draped walls to soften the construction, and given personality with many of my own things.

Atlanta Homes & Lifestyles then invited me to participate in the Southeastern Designer Show House two years running. The challenge here was how to make a large-scale space—the primary bedroom—function comfortably. The answer? Divide and conquer, in this case with a sitting room and a sleeping space in calm, soothing colors, with touches of blush. My second go-round, I decorated a study that became, for me, a composition in shapes and contrast.

In the 2016 *Traditional Home*'s Southern Style Now, I went even more graphically rogue, covering the walls and ceiling of a guest bedroom in the same pattern, and adding woven baskets galore.

But 2017 was my year of the show house thanks to O'More, *Atlanta Home & Lifestyles*, and Kips Bay New York, which was a career pinnacle and a turning point—I got a cover-boy moment in the *New York Times* Style section. I worked with MJ Atelier to create an all-white and off-black fantasia that climbed the stairwell walls from the entry to the second-floor landing, and our hand-piped plaster on linen installation brought the flora

PRECEDING OVERLEAF: I like to dress for the occasion, and nothing says New York more than basic black with timeless white. RIGHT: At the Kips Bay Show House 2017, the stairway's existing iron scrollwork was the catalyst for the high-contrast silhouettes that made the custom stairwell wall treatment created with MJ Atelier so distinctive. The pattern brought a taste of Tennessee's distinctive flora and fauna to the Big Apple. Mirrored archways intensified the depth of the drama. Painted a light blue, the light well on high hovered over all like the dome of the sky.

and fauna of Tennessee to the big city, big time. For Kips Bay Palm Beach 2020, my challenge was the outdoor pavilion, which presented an opportunity to test some new ideas about what makes an outdoor room a gracious living space. For me, the answer here was teak and white furnishings that let the greens of nature pop.

But the 2022 *House Beautiful* Show House in Atlanta has been so far the most interesting learning experience of all, because it involved three spaces, not just one. This gave me an opportunity to refine my most recent ideas about creating rooms that entice people in, connect in spirit, but remain distinct in look. The entry, lacquered in a warm, rich red, gives people a hug as they enter. The combination living and dining room—we called it the dining lounge—wrapped in a deep teal, is an informal but stylish entertaining space that keeps people at the front of the house. The powder room, in slate gray with a grooved architectural screen we created, is functional chic that both stands out in fabulousness but also ties into the other two spaces.

While the evolution of my aesthetic is visible across the decade, my focus is always straight ahead—and on paying the benefits of beauty forward.

OPPOSITE AND BELOW: A bedroom for *Atlanta Homes & Lifestyles'* Southeastern Designer Showhouse gave me an opportunity to demonstrate how an oversized guest bedroom can also serve as an optional place for lounging as well as sleeping. The goal was to give the space a feminine graciousness while keeping it tailored. The wallpaper is my Shatter design from Carleton V.

OPPOSITE AND ABOVE: *House Beautiful*'s Whole Home 2022 offered each participant a cluster of rooms to transform as an opportunity to make a significant statement of decorative intention. Mine were the foyer, living room, and main powder room. In a decision to go big or go home, I drenched the front entry in two shades of red lacquer for warmth and drama. The large painting by George Williams, mesmerizing on its own, also hinted at the forms and colors to come. Rested on a white oak cabinet opposite the gold-leafed chair, the painting's placement suggested a casual, even intimate comfort with art itself. The pinstriped detailing common to both pieces of furniture encouraged the conversation between these two areas of the space. The art over the chair is by Nashville's Jennifer Gibbs.

The living room became a chance to tell a story about flexibility and show what it means to create a space in the front of the home that serves multiple functions—specifically living, dining, and games. Wrapped in medium teal, the room became a luxurious cocoon of comfort. The Ekstrem chair—a 1984 design from Norway—inserted its bold eccentricity and contrasting color into the mix. The George Williams painting over the mantel created a line of cohesion with the foyer.

OPPOSITE: The Vale London curtain fabric united all three spaces through color and pattern. The table of my own design walked the line between dining and games. ABOVE: Phillip Jeffries's ombré paper with the console from Grothouse provided a rest for the eyes. The lighting is from Visual Comfort. OVERLEAF LEFT: The powder room's Arte wallpaper completed the greige. Flooring is from Ann Sacks; the counter on the floating vanity is by Caesarstone. OVERLEAF RIGHT: A laser-cut metal screen from Architectural Grille in Brooklyn became a privacy panel. The painting is by Nashville-based artist Jennifer Gibbs.

ACKNOWLEDGMENTS

It's been such a privilege to compile the contents of this book, and there are many people to thank for being part of my design career and projects thus far. Stay tuned for more to come!

To my incredible clients, thank you for trusting in me and my design vision. It's an absolute pleasure to create interiors that meet your aesthetic—an honor that I never take for granted.

My deepest appreciation and heartfelt gratitude to the following:

O'More School of Design, education is everything. You gave me the foundation and skills to go out into the design world and create. I am honored that you invited me onto your Board of Directors.

Bennett Galleries, and especially Elizabeth for always helping us select the most outstanding curated frames for our clients' art.

Briana Doherty for all that you do to make certain that the daily tasks are completed to perfection. You are a true taskmaster.

James Dunn of Vintage Millworks for creating fantastic millwork specifically for my clients' homes.

Jay Frazer for your expert moving skills and being an integral part of our team every step—and mile—of the way.

Todd Greene for figuring out a way to curate and precisely place our clients' art in the most special way.

The late Albert Hadley, for your life in design. I am so proud to have known you and am thankful that introduced me to David Kleinberg, one of the greatest talents in the design industry.

Dennis Hunt of Ainsworth-Noah Showroom, no matter the time of day or night, for always being there to solve a problem and be of help!

Jerry Kemp and the team at Kemp Wallcoverings for your professionalism and help all these years. Without you, our projects would be much less rich, layered, and interesting.

Mary and Joe Lannom for the unbelievable marble and stone details that wouldn't be possible without you.

Jody Malone for your ability to realize our vision for the custom carpets that are the foundations of the rooms we create.

Lisa Simpkin from Blanche Field, LLC, for your collaboration and creativity with couture lampshades beyond compare.

Holly Trepka for always making sure everything is organized to a T.

Zina Studios for your outstanding designs that always add a touch of special to our clients' walls. Thank you for letting me use your pattern "Square Deal" on the inside covers of this book.

The unbelievable drapery and blinds workrooms we work with time and time again. Your approach is always integral to our projects.

The fabric and furniture companies that produce my designs and showcase them in your collections. Carleton V Ltd., Ironware International, and Keith Fritz Fine Furniture, I am honored to be a member of your families.

The architectural firms we have collaborated with over the years, and especially Jonathan Torode. Working with you is always a true pleasure.

Douglas Friedman, Emily Followill, Robert Peterson, Zeke Ruelas, Blake Ross, and Julie Ross. Seeing my work through your lenses is the best kind of education. Without your photography talents, this book would not be possible.

Anita Sarsidi for transforming images with your special touch.

The late Jane Freeze Sloan, your floral talents were one in a million. I miss you every day. Always have flowers!

All the editors of the many magazines that have included us in their pages over the years; your features have led to our success, and we couldn't be more grateful.

Two premier design industry professional organizations—Leaders of Design and Design Leadership Network. Through my membership you have opened opportunities and facilitated introductions to some of the finest designers and vendors in the world.

Madge Baird and the entire Gibbs Smith team for this opportunity to publish my first book.

Judith Nasatir for taking my words and constructing them in the most precise, expressive way.

Doug Turshen and Steve Turner for making my vision of this book come to life.

My employees past and present for the time we've had together creating beautiful homes.

Robert Brown for being my design buddy and for hitting the flea markets, showrooms, and expos with me all these years. There's no one I'd rather travel the world with.

Sebastian Varney for your words of wisdom. You have encouraged me to grow and build my business from the very beginning.

Nazira Handal, the queen of the Kips Bay Show House, for your support. It's been a true joy getting to know and work with you on Kips Bay New York in 2017 and Kips Bay Palm Beach in 2020 and 2024.

Randi Stovesand for being you. You've always been my biggest cheerleader, dearest friend, and trusted confidant. There's no way I can adequately describe my gratitude.

John Mark Windle for your treasured friendship, advice, knowledge, and for being a sounding board!

Tinnie A. Clay for organizing my life and keeping me in line. Your dedication to me personally and professionally is cherished. My family and I love you and all that you do, especially Artie!

Brad Wensel for your steadfast support and encouragement. Since we met, you've been with me every step of the way. You've believed in my success since I started my business. You are part of my life and of this company.

It's impossible to name all the people who have helped and encouraged me along the way because the list goes on and on. But you know who you are—and I know who you are—and you have my boundless gratitude.

Text © 2024 Jonathan Savage

Photographs © 2024 as follows:

Douglas Friedman: front cover. 1, 19, 20, 28–29, 33–35, 37–39, 42–45, 49, 51–53, 60, 62–63, 68–79, 82–89, 91–93, 95–97, 102–19, 136, 138–39, 141–47, 150–57, 226–27

Emily Followill: back cover, 17, 22–25, 46–48, 54–55, 57–59, 228–29, 240

Robert Peterson: 2, 230–37

Zeke Ruelas: 5, 26–27, 197–223

Blake Ross and Julie Ross: 6–7, 13–15, 30–31, 41, 64–65, 67, 80–81, 94, 98–101, 140, 148–49, 158–81, 182–95, 239

James Belston: 121–35

Marco Ricca: 8, 224

End sheets: "Square Deal," courtesy Zina Studios

First Edition
28 27 26 25 24   5 4 3 2 1

Published by
Gibbs Smith
PO Box 667
Layton, Utah 84040
1.800.835.4993 orders
www.gibbs-smith.com

Designed by Doug Turshen with Steve Turner

Library of Congress Control Number: 2023951899
ISBN: 978-1-4236-6523-6

Printed and bound in China
Gibbs Smith books are printed on FSC-certified paper

PRECEDING OVERLEAF: Art and fashion, which live at the center of this client's world, were the forces of gravity and levity in her primary bedroom. The painting is by Ted Faiers.

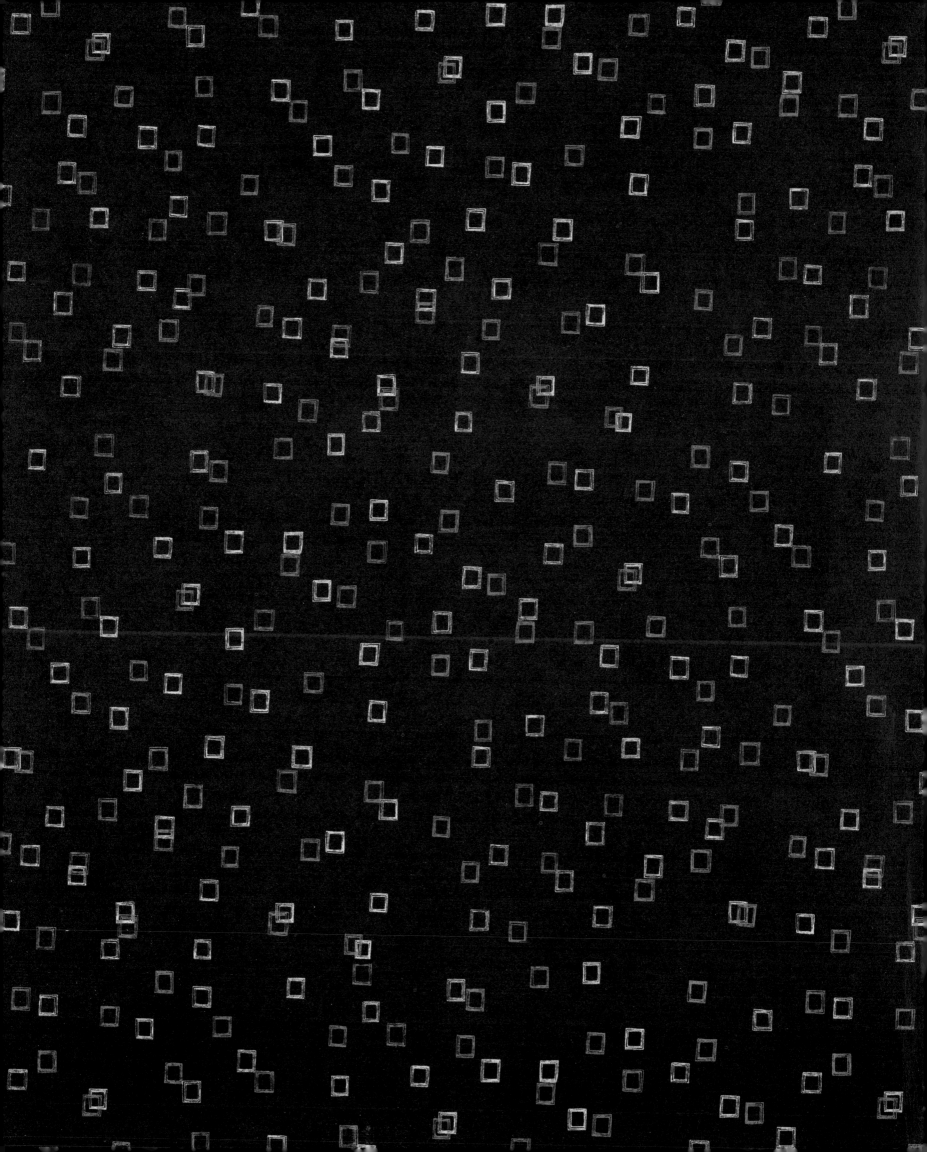